How to Make People
Laugh

Discover How to Be Funny and Improve Your Sense of Humor

by Jeffrey Mason

Table of Contents

Introduction

You're either funny or you're not, right? Well, not exactly.

One of the biggest misconceptions about being funny is that you are either a natural-born comedian or you can't tell a joke to save your life. The truth of the matter is that being funny is a talent, and like any other talent or skill, it can either be developed or neglected. Ask any stand-up comedian, and they'll likely have a story to tell you how their first few performances were absolute nightmares. They didn't know how to engage the audience, and they didn't yet have their timing and delivery all worked out. Even people who feel called to be funny, or who are perhaps naturally funny, still have much to learn about the nature of humor before it seems easy to them.

In this book you'll learn the fundamental principles of good humor. You'll also learn how to summon the proper energy and charisma to keep people entertained and laughing. If you're ready to be the life of the party in a comfortable and easy way, then read on!

Chapter 1: How to Pleasantly Upset Your Audience

This chapter will address the raw essentials of humor, the why and how of laughter. If you're not interested in theory and would like to immediately get down to the how-to's of being funny, then you may want to skip ahead to chapter 2.

Laughter is the body's psycho-emotional response to a disarmed threat. As an example, I'll tell you a quick story that happened a few weeks ago.

An old college buddy of mine, Lisa, was visiting my house for dinner to catch up on old times and what have you, and after we were done eating, she excused herself to go to the bathroom. Seconds later, I heard a loud scream, so I came running – only to find her standing on the toilet seat, freaking out because she saw a huge spider next to the trash can. Recognizing that this was a fake spider Halloween toy that my niece had been playing with yesterday (and I had attempted to throw away after she left – but apparently missed the trash can), I decided to play along in an effort to be funny.

I told Lisa to stay put, and I ran back to the kitchen and got a jar. When I came back, I pretended to attempt to capture the spider with the jar, and in doing so, I used the jar edge to manipulate the fake spider into looking like it was moving and thus making its capture more difficult. Finally, I let out a wild painful yelp, screaming "It bit me! And got away!" which only caused Lisa to panic even more, almost losing balance on the toilet seat. That's when I looked up, smiled, and held the fake spider up for her to see it wasn't a real threat at all, but it was just a Halloween prop.

This realization inspired her to release absolute spontaneous and uncontrollable laughter. And as funny as I believe myself to be, the laughter had nothing to do with my acting performance. Her laughter was solely based on the psycho-emotional relief that she experienced from realizing that the very threat that started this all was disarmed; that the spider was not real. This is the way in which laughter can be an expression of relief from a potentially threatening circumstance.

Now, if you're having a hard time getting your head around how all jokes begin as threats, consider the hypothesis in the context of Jay Leno's famous "Headlines" segment. This is the segment where Mr. Leno reads newspaper headlines containing amusing misspellings, grammatical errors, or simply unfortunate phrasings such as "Reeding tutors needed" or "Weight gain helped Butt stand out." The only reason Leno's bit is funny is because these headlines are taken from an actual printed publication (usually a newspaper). During the segment, Leno shows us the physical clippings. If he didn't show us the physical evidence, then the segment wouldn't strike us as funny. Think about it. Without the physical evidence, we wouldn't be forced to absorb a threat to our preconceived idea of a newspaper, as a distinguished entity teeming with accomplished writers and editors, a paragon of grammatical propriety and tactful phrasings, delivering us the news of the day. It is the violation of our subconscious preconception of what a newspaper should be that drives home the humor of "Headlines." What allows Leno's audience to react with pleasure—through laughter—rather than with fear or anxiety is the simple assurance we have that strange news headlines, though disruptive, are not threatening. They are but fake spiders lurking near our trash cans.

Being funny is the work of disruption and playful exposition. If you want to make people laugh you need to find cracks in their preconceived ideas and disrupt them in a way that is provoking but ultimately non-threatening. Many people accomplish this using *sarcasm* and *deadpan humor*.

Sarcasm is the playful (and, if misused, snootish) asserting of seriousness to a subject matter in clear defiance of another person's expected or normal perception. A child who doesn't like broccoli is being sarcastic when he tells his mother playfully (or snootishly) "Yeah, Mom, let's have broccoli every night this week. In fact, let's grow broccoli in the back yard while we're at it." If you want to make people laugh, well-placed sarcasm can be a valuable tool.

Deadpan humor is essentially sarcasm with a "dead pan" delivery. Deadpan essentially entails a monotone voice and an air of bored indifference. Sometimes deadpan humor baffles people because they're not always completely sure you're joking, which, unless you're Andy Kauffman, can be a bit problematic. A good example of deadpan humor can be found in Ben Stein's performance in Ferris Bueller's day off. Ferris Bueller is absent from the attendance roll call, and Stein's droning voice, "Bueller, Bueller" and the silence that ensues is the stuff of legend.

Chapter 2: Don't Be Afraid to Be Un-funny

Have you ever been in a classroom or a meeting and noticed that someone else is making everyone laugh? And, worst of all, he's doing it using virtually the exact same commentary you had brewing in your brain but were too shy to blurt out.

Being funny and being shy really, really don't mix. A funny person is outspoken and risk-taking. You don't have to be a loud-mouth, who is constantly monopolizing conversations. Nor should you come across as a validation seeking loser trying too hard to make people like him. You do, however, have to put yourself out there and risk facing that uncomfortable silence after something you thought was funny lands on deaf ears. A funny person seizes her moment without overthinking the circumstances. When it comes to something as abstract as humor, there's always a way to analyze your way out of an attempt at being funny. Don't succumb to over-analyzing. Let your audience do the analysis and let *them* come back with the "funny or not" verdict. No one should fault you for trying.

The "DO NOT ABORT" Rule:

A good rule of thumb is to always finish and fully express your thoughts once you begin to articulate them. In other words, if you've consciously or subconsciously processed something to an extent where your brain has triggered your mouth to begin working towards vocal expression, *do not abort*! Go with it. A comedian is the opposite of a politician, in that a comedian minimizes self-censorship.

Going back to what was mentioned in the introduction: It is the normal and natural experience of professional comedians to fall short (or totally bomb) on their first several attempts to entertain an audience. There's nothing wrong with that. But even at the casual level, being a funny person requires a willingness to endure failed attempts at humor. If you persevere and get through these rough patches, your reward will be well worth it.

Chapter 3: Timing and Delivery

As in writing, comedy requires an awareness of how people process information. To make people laugh you must develop a sense for how things are heard and processed by your audience. *Comedic Timing* is the use of rhythm, pace and tempo to enhance comedic delivery.

One very simple but often under-utilized element of comedic timing is the *pause*. To make people laugh, you must learn where and how to pause in your delivery. Usually, a pause is used to give the audience a chance to absorb information for a set up. If your punch line involves an acrobatic play on words, a pause can be used to give the audience a chance to put the joke together, to "get it." Audiences love it when they have to work just a little (not too much), to "get" a joke. It makes them feel invested in the joke and their laughter thus becomes not only an approval and validation of your comedic genius, but of their own as well.

Pauses can also be used to heighten the suspense before a punch line. Let's say you've got a really wacky story about your recent visit to the dentist that culminates in a clever one-liner you wrote that sums up your unique take on the whole experience. Your description of the visit would be your lead up; the story should amuse the audience in and of itself by offering a relatable and interesting account. And just before your one-liner punch line, pause for a moment.

"I paid my bill and was about to leave when I burped up this horrible battery-acid taste in my mouth. I saw there was a lady in the waiting room. I felt I really should warn her." …..*Pause*……

Your pause here will leave the audience poised for your one-liner/punch line.

Timing can also be put to use by being aware of the speed of your delivery. Some things should be said quickly and others more slowly. If you're trying to be funny, don't ever needlessly hurry through a joke and risk giving the impression that what you're saying isn't interesting or important. However, if there's a good reason to use faster delivery to de-emphasize a certain element of your joke or routine, then sure, go for it. A good example of fast-paced delivery can be found in George Carlin's famous "Seven Words You Can't Say On Television" routine, in which he purposefully and continuously speeds through a reiteration of the seven "dirty words" that are not allowed on the public airwaves, while slowing his pace down through an ensuing scholarly analysis of why these seven words aren't as bad as the world would have us believe.

Comedic timing is also important in physical or *slapstick* comedy. The bucket of water never falls on Charlie Chaplin's head until the perfect moment.

Chapter 4: Where to Get (and Not to Get) New Material

A great way to become funnier is to expand your range of personal life experiences. The more unique and diverse your experiences, the more angles on life you'll have to inspect. And don't worry, in a comedic sense, being well versed on the affairs of the world is not all that difficult. You want to experience and learn about things that a lot of people experience and know about. This will allow you to better relate to your audience. For example, the experience of dating, having a girlfriend, a wife, and/or children all are very common and simple experiences that allow you to find common "funny" ground on which to relate to the audience if you choose to include some of these experiences in your subject matter.

Another great place to start is pop culture. Not everyone enjoys indulging in Hollywood gossip pages, but some of us certainly do. If you're one of those people then you're going to love the "research component" of being a comedian. You need to soak it all up, news, random trivia, and every slimy ounce of pop-culture malarkey that slivers out of the sewer. This will keep you up to date and armed with relatable material that people are eager to laugh at.

During your hunt for new material, be careful how much you take from other comedians. You don't want to be caught, even in a very informal situation, mimicking someone else's routine without giving them credit. Now, for simple jokes, that's a little different. Jokes lend themselves to borrowing, trading, and sharing, but don't try and pass off personals stories and routines that aren't your own unless you acknowledge their original author. Everything in moderation; it's ok to be inspired by other comedians and to incorporate bits and pieces from their work into your own, but at the end of the day, your humor should be distinct to you. It will come off as a lot more natural that way and you'll ultimately be funnier for it.

Chapter 5: Tapping into a Continuous Stream of Laughter

There's an old campfire game that perfectly illustrates the contagious nature of laughter in a group.

The participants sit in a circle around the campfire. The game begins with two people sitting opposite from one another picking an animal and attempting to do an imitation of that animal. The other participants shout out their guesses at which animals are being imitated. Once a participant guesses the correct animal, he must do an imitation of that same animal laughing (the one he just guessed correctly – for example, a laughing goat). After the first participant's animal is guessed, she stops her imitation and the person sitting to her left begins to imitate an animal of her choice. Anyone who is not already imitating an animal continues guessing (usually while laughing uncontrollably) until only one person is left not doing an imitation of a laughing-version of an animal.

What you will find in this game is that it never reaches its ordained completion point. Usually after the third or fourth participant is trying to imitate the laughter of a goldfish or a giraffe, the entire scene has devolved wonderfully into an electric unstoppable melee of laughter.

Laughter, like fire, is self-perpetuating, and needs only a steady source of fuel to keep it going. If your goal is to make people laugh, then you must learn to cultivate this self-perpetuating atmosphere. Here are a few tips:

Lighten the mood:

Keep a positive, upbeat and friendly mood in your social environments. You can do this by simply being a positive and upbeat person who doesn't take himself too seriously.

Make Sure Your Own Laugh is Cheerful and Not Distracting:

Some people are cursed with an obnoxious laugh. If you're not careful, your laugh can become its own punchline. If you've got a laugh that would make Fran Dresher cringe, you might want to do what you can to rein it in a bit. Practice makes perfect.

Be Confident:

Confidence can go a long way in enhancing your creativity and asserting your funny takes on life in a way that will make people naturally want to respond. Confidence is also key to the execution of self-deprecating humor that doesn't create awkwardness.

Be Selective About Your Environments:

If you're a nurse or a doctor, then you probably don't want to spend too much time trying to be funny when you're discussing the rapidly spreading cancer affecting the lymph nodes of the patient in room 202. Now, that said, a sketch piece featuring a screwball MD trying way too hard to be funny under totally inappropriate circumstances is a winner indeed. But in general, you should recognize venues where you can strive to be the life of the party and other venues where you're best off keeping things low key.

Adopt a Mischievous Attitude:

An important technical term in comedy is the *target*, aka the thing being goofed on during a comedic performance. Targets can be audience members, celebrities, shopping malls, your own weight issues, anything really. A good comedian is prone to poking and prodding at her targets, trying to mine out comedic gems. Therefore, a comedian can make good use out of a mischievous attitude, a playful impish spirit looking to stir things up a bit and perhaps get into some trouble. Remember however to proceed with caution and be mindful of the audience at-hand. It may not be the best idea to cruise into a biker bar to try out your routine. Try a close group of friends first.

Research and read a lot of Jokes:

Lawyers and doctors aren't above keeping a joke folder stashed on their computer to use at parties, business meetings, what have you. One of the easiest, most surefire ways to be funny is to be a person who knows some really good jokes. Jokes are great for injecting life back into a conversation once it's gone stale. They're also great for getting people in good moods for sales pitches or negotiating. You don't have to memorize and recite the jokes you read word for word, just know the essentials and practice telling them.

Chapter 6: The Man with the Funny Reputation

If you continuously delight others with your wit and humor, you will soon develop a reputation for being funny. This will only happen though if you stay true to yourself and don't try and be another person. Many times people, younger people especially, make this mistake. They're in awe of a classmate or friend who always seems to be cracking everyone up and they wonder why they can't do the same. So they try to imitate this classmate only to find out that they just can't pull it off on a consistent basis.

Funny people come in a variety of shapes, sizes and styles. Find out who you are and where you harbor your most noteworthy comedic strengths. If you have a chance, network and associate with other comics and talk shop. Just like anything else, it is possible to totally nerd out on comedy. Timing, venue, audience investment, bombing, these are things that comics tend to enjoy discussing with one another.

It's important too to be aware of the dark side of comedy. Comedy creates laughter which is healing and uplifting, but by its very nature, comedy carries a kind of destructive energy. It is the duty of comedy and comedians to make us question our assumptions and see our world in new and interesting ways. This involves breaking down and attacking the norms of the day. This can also involve attacking other people, whether they deserve it or not, even if it's only in humor and jest. This is the dark but proper ethos of comedy. Many comedians, more so than in other professions, battle with depression and substance abuse. Not to say that it's not possible to be a happy, healthy, *and* funny person, but you may need to anticipate visiting some pretty dark places as you progress.

But enough about the darkness of comedy. It's also very true that people simply like other people who are funny. If you're looking to make friends or get more dates, being funny can certainly help. In terms of dating in particular, having a good sense of humor can be a total difference maker. Laughter calms tense situations, like first dates, and allows people to drop their guard and open up a bit more. Not to mention, for guys especially, the ability to command the attention of a group is seen by women as an incredibly attractive trait.

It's good to have a reputation as being funny. It's much better than having a reputation as being boring. No joke.

Conclusion

Being funny is a great advantage to your social life. That's probably why you originally decided to read this book. If you're looking to improve your social skills by using humor, however, you need to be firing on all of your other social cylinders as well. Be sure you're taking good care of yourself physically and work on being a confident secure person that people love to be around. Good general social traits make it all the more likely that people will be responsive to your sense of humor, whatever that may be.

Another important lesson to take away from this book is to never lose yourself in your pursuit of comedic talent. Don't try and be someone else, but instead let your best and craziest versions of yourself shine through in your humor. Great comics are great because there's simply no one else like them. There never will be another Jim Carrey or Robin Williams, and there will never be another person with your unique brand of humor either.

Remember to study and perfect your timing and pacing and to use pauses for emphasis. Mastering these technical elements especially will require practice and commitment, so don't get discouraged if you don't knock 'em dead the first time out of the gates. No matter where you're starting from or what level of natural talent you have, a good sense of humor *can* be developed and improved upon over time.

Study the greats. Go back in time a bit and check out some old Lenny Bruce and Sam Kinison stand up. Notice what material feels dated or time specific and what material would still hold up well today. Remember, it's ok to take influence from your favorite comics, just don't try to become them.

Continually seek out new and interesting life experiences that will provide fodder for your comedic pursuits. Put yourself in uncomfortable situations. Carry a notebook and catalog your observations. When you're writing out your routine, be sure to put yourself in the position of your audience members, hearing this material for the first time. Pay attention to the pace and sequence of delivery. Remember also to become a pop-culture freak. You need to be first in line at Perez Hilton's next book signing. Subscribe to pop-culture blogs, youtube channels, and RSS feeds. Follow the career of Miley Cyrus and Kim Kardashian.

Start a new file on your computer, or a new page on your mobile device notepad app, and call it "Jokes." Go ahead and add three right now. Just find three good jokes on the internet—Chuck Norris comes to mind—and write them or paste them into your file. Read through the jokes a few times until you've got their gist committed to memory. Now you know three more jokes than you knew before you began reading this book. Congratulations! Next up, be on the lookout for opportunities to whip them out in social settings, or even when hanging out with a buddy. Try them a few different times (with different audiences), using different timing and delivery methods, and see which get the best reaction. Become a student of your own craft this way.

Understand what comedy is. It is an ultimately benign destruction of our pretensions and preconceived notions. Committing yourself to comedy can lead you down a dark psychological path, as is evidenced in the stories of so many exceptional comedic talents. Protect yourself from the dark side by brushing your teeth three times a day and getting at least 7.5 hours of sleep every night. Seriously though, take care of yourself if you decide to dive deep into the universe of comedy. Or if you choose not to take care of yourself, at least integrate your self-destructive out-of-control lifestyle into your comedy routine, and let us marvel and gawk at your personal tragedy.

Finally, I'd like to thank you for purchasing this book! Follow my advice and never give up, and I can assure you that you'll be splitting people's sides in no time! If you enjoyed the book or found it helpful, I'd greatly appreciate it if you'd take a moment to leave a review on Amazon. Thank you!

12982645R00023

Printed in Great Britain
by Amazon